MY TAROT

MY TAROT

Something Else

NISHA MEHTA

PARTRIDGE

ISBN: Hardcover   978-1-4828-7373-3
                 Softcover   978-1-4828-7372-6
                 eBook   978-1-4828-7371-9

Print information available on the last page.

To order additional copies of this book, contact
Partridge India
000 800 10062 62
orders.india@partridgepublishing.com

www.partridgepublishing.com/india

CONTENTS

FLASHBACK

How it started.

Today: 5th January 2014

I was talking with a client about another who had written a book and wanted to have it published.

In the conversation, a suggestion was made that I write my own book on Tarot relating it with the different aspects of colors, feng shui, numerology, astrology, spirituality and material life. That I would get all the backing, help and support to get it to the finishing line.

And here I am, already writing about it at night, 10.25 pm while this conversation happened exactly 6 hours ago.

I remember filling my profile on a social website some 8 or 9 years ago stating that my favorite book would be the one I author.

6 years ago, I started writing about a card thinking that finally the time to pursue writing my own book has come, however I ended up tearing the paper. It was a description of a card - *10 of Wands*

I have been professionally practising tarot since 2002 and as a hobby since 1997 where I would use playing cards to predict events of the future. I gave up after the shock for indirectly predicting the death of a very dear friend. I remember my words to him *I cannot see you after May, it's all black* I later realized that I have a gift, I see images and pictures and am told by an inner voice about the timing of events. My friend died on 31st March. A slight confusion in hearing the timing. (March and May)

Curiosity made me pick up a tarot deck in 2001. After reading it, I realized that we can follow remedies and work on solutions to bring about positive changes in our lives, if we know about situations in advance. The need to help people get through difficult patches of their lives made me learn more about cards, colors, days, phases of sun and moon, witch craft, paganism, candle magic, spells, numbers, planets, astrology, feng shui, magic and anything related to occult and spirituality. Having studied child psychology was a boon to me and helped me with counseling. I started working on solutions and remedies, experimenting on myself. Seeing the absolute results I got from them, it just became a profession then on.

I had the means to bring changes to those who came to me for help. The Universe was guiding me to do what I did best. There was a time I mocked astrologers and those who would read birth charts. Today I am doing the same. Destiny has a simple way of teaching us not to look down upon anything without knowing about it completely.

I learned that any art has a dual effect and can be used to harm others or help them. I made a choice to make a living and get blessings by helping others through my art and natural ability as psychic and medium.

One local magazine sent me a questionnaire where I was asked: "Who inspired me?" My reply: the ones who cheat and demean others are my inspiration to ***not*** be like them.

My path has not been smooth, with people demoralizing me, calling me names and even cheating me. There were times I crumbled and was on the verge of giving up. I did too. But the challenge of surviving and coming out as a winner was stronger. I wanted to be able to restore faith in people who had started to believe that genuine help is out-of-date nowadays.

I have studied many decks, own quite a few, burned some of them, thrown some & torn others when I felt that the energies were not working for me. I wish to portray the knowledge of all these as well as my personal experiences of readings to make it easier for the beginner to grasp as much as possible with ease and without having to study too many decks.

Intuitively, I was guided to study tarot with reference to peoples' date of birth, numerology and planets which took me a step further in my quest in understanding the cards.

Being a clay artist & having worked with interiors, I knew the importance of placing certain objects and pictures in their right direction to get maximum benefits by enhancing the environment, I combined this knowledge with tarot to help give my clients everything they needed at one place, through my readings.

Where I was a disbeliever in astrology, I even made efforts to learn to read the birth charts and horoscopes in order to understand how I can apply it in my tarot readings. I asked a client to tutor me with basic significance of the birth chart. I still have a long way to go and many untouched tarot decks to study but this is the time I need to put my inputs in the Universe and give the knowledge back that I have picked up from people and space.

I have been a beginner and we all have to start somewhere. I am making it easy for everyone with my book to make that start.

I pray that I shall be guided in the right direction with blessings!

INTRODUCTION

When you approach any medium or oracle, you go there with a preconceived notion that you will get all the answers to your questions as per your liking. You must also be open to understanding that some things are not supposed to be revealed and you need to go through certain experiences for your own growth process.

There are some cards in tarot that sound mysterious and do not reveal everything you want to know. At this time, you use the cards to know if all will be well and you will be protected during this phase.

This will confirm your belief that ***Tarot tells you what you need to know and not what you want to know***

My Tarot -
"Something Else"

Why *My Tarot-Something Else*?

Everyone needs to relate to "something else" that they own or possess. I am sure that going through this book will make people relate to a lot of things said and unsaid, bring back memories or associate their lives with the card meanings and the simple solutions written as *Something Else*

I am going to present matter to you in a simplified form. After reading about 25 decks related to Tarot and Oracles, Runes and I Ching; I realized I did not have the energy and patience to read and grasp any more, I just wanted specifics that could make a difference to me and my readings so people who consulted me could benefit. I want this book to make a difference to you, bring out the best in you or remove the worst too.

Let your voice be a translator of your soul's feelings when you see the card picked by you. The knowledge in this book can be referred to while using any deck. Intuition plays an important role, listening to your own feelings will make a reading exceptional and authentic.

WHY TAROT IS DEPENDABLE?

Our soul has all the answers that we seek. It is only a matter of going within to search for them. However, we live on a physical plane where most of the time, it becomes difficult for us to believe in our own inner voice which we call intuition. We have learned to believe only what we see and require tangible proof for it.

Cards act as a bridge between the known and the unknown. For example: You allow your soul to connect with the right message when you pull the cards by a vibe that makes you choose any specific card. These cards look the same when kept face down. It is only when you open the cards after you have taken them out from the pack that you see what is drawn by you.

Tarot - Break
Up Of Cards

Tarot Cards are divided into the Major and Minor Arcana which signify certain type of events in our lives.

Cards of *Major **Arcana* relate to major life events that are set and have very little scope for alteration. When they appear in any reading, they signify a change in your life, a new phase or point to some very important and significant situation. They are numbered from 0 to 21.

Cards of *Minor **Arcana* relate to the daily events in your lives and efforts can be made to bring a change in your Major life cycle by making changes on a day to day basis. Knowing about smaller details will allow you to take remedial measures for the future.

** ARCANA

Arcana means secrets. The Tarot holds the secret, not only to your queries but also embodies Universal secrets, scriptures and knowledge of ancient and traditional values that you need to imbibe in your lives. Tarot is a complete guideline of how life is lived. It depicts the journey of The Fool.

Minor *Arcana* are represented by 4 Suits with 14 cards each → 10 pips cards + 4 court cards.

The numbered cards denote events in your lives and the Court Cards could represent you, people in your life or events.

The 4 Suits of the Minor *Arcana*(Wands, Pentacles, Cups, Swords) have their own properties, elements and characteristic.

TAROT CARDS

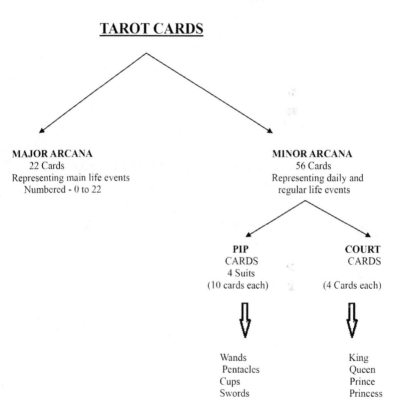

MAJOR ARCANA
22 Cards
Representing main life events
Numbered - 0 to 22

MINOR ARCANA
56 Cards
Representing daily and
regular life events

PIP
CARDS
4 Suits
(10 cards each)

COURT
CARDS

(4 Cards each)

Wands
Pentacles
Cups
Swords

King
Queen
Prince
Princess

THE MAJOR ARCANA

Life events which are influenced by your karma over a long period of time come under the major arcana. These cards represent situations that affect you over a long period of time, months, years or even lifetimes.

There are some events that are unavoidable and most of them are represented in the major arcana.

These cards can also relate to your birth chart, horoscope and zodiac which requires deeper study.

The images for the major arcana in My Tarot-Something Else could be used for meditation to relieve you from any confusion you are facing and help in understanding a card better.

The one-liners and punch lines are also effective when repeated as positive affirmations for your emotional and holistic well being.

FOOL

Punch: When your destination is confirmed, a path will appear, the journey will begin.

Advice: Trust is an important factor here, trusting the Highest Being and knowing that you are looked after will give you the ability to move on and take steps towards your goals.

Something Else: Put your hands over your heart, breathe deeply and repeat the words *I trust you*. Do this for 22 days and see the change in yourself and those around you.

Magician

Punch: The greatest magic is when you attune yourself with the Universe to do your bidding, not waiting for people to follow your instructions.

Advice: Muster your willpower to complete tasks and unfinished projects. Be careful, there are people trying to trick you or guide you on a wrong path.

Something Else: Watch a magic show, for real or online. Believe that your life is magical too.

HIGH PRIESTESS

The answer to the
mysteries of the
Universe lie within the
pillars of
THE HIGH PRIESTESS

Punch: Where there is mystery, there is definite curiosity.

Advice: Know and understand your own potentials. Before working on your issues, know what you have to offer so that you will be able to gauge the complete depth of the situation you are in.

Something Else: Try solving a puzzle, get a cube game and work on sorting it. Know that while solving the game puzzle, your real life issues are sorting themselves out too.

Empress

THE EMPRESS' secret to abundance is harvesting and sharing her good fortunes !

Punch: Growth and success matter when everything around you flourishes and prospers.

Advice: Nurture and care for all that needs attention, wish everyone well, it will bring you back a lot of good wishes in return.

Something Else: Get plants, nurture them. If you have the space & time for gardening, go for it.

EMPEROR

Punch: Experience toughens. Love mellows.

Advice: Rigidity comes from hard times and a tough past. Discuss with others before taking tough decisions. Involving others will reduce your burden.

Something Else: Go out and party, time to loosen up.

HIEROPHANT

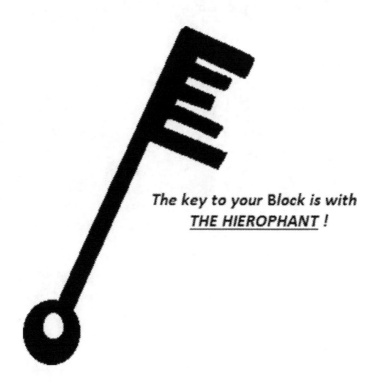

The key to your Block is with
THE HIEROPHANT !

Punch: Tradition is not always boring.

Advice: Follow the known method designed by ancestors. There is always some meaning in culture and tradition even in modern times.

Something Else: Go to a spiritual holy place and offer prayers. Look into your family ancestral history.

LOVERS

Punch: If your choices determine your destination, how can destiny be fixed?

Advice: Decisions need to be made that will determine the outcome of your situation. Your partner/friend/companion needs attention, do not lose focus of your relationships.

Something Else: Reconnect with family and friends. Pick up that communication thread you lost over a period of time and begin again.

CHARIOT

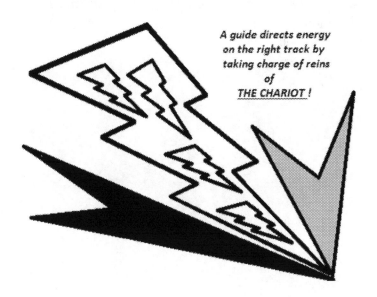

A guide directs energy
on the right track by
taking charge of reins
of
THE CHARIOT !

Punch: When you don't take charge, you will be controlled.

Advice: A situation needs your attention even if your mind seems to be diverted with other issues. Get a grip over yourself and take charge. The situation demands it.

Something Else: Evaluate your life. Make notes, either mentally or on paper to know what needs your immediate attention.

STRENGTH

Power is the outcome of spiritual STRENGTH !

Punch: Your belief is your greatest power.

Advice: Pay attention to your feelings. Go for your aims and targets, you will achieve them through your spiritual and mental will, not by physical force.

Something Else: Write the word Power (with black marker) on a piece of paper and look at it everyday for a few minutes. Then close your eyes and feel yourself as a strong, powerful person.

HERMIT

All questions are
never instantly
answered by
THE HERMIT !

Punch: The answer lies with you, you just need to reach within to seek clarity.

Advice: Learn to be guided by signs, trust that the Universe will show you the way, you need to approach it with an attitude to receive It's blessings. Be a learner & guidance will be given to you, one way or another.

Something Else: Before going to bed, pray and ask the Universe to send you signs about your desire. Do this for 9 consecutive nights. You will get a sign, sooner or later.

WHEEL OF FORTUNE

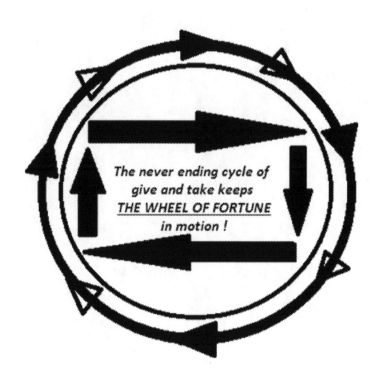

The never ending cycle of
give and take keeps
THE WHEEL OF FORTUNE
in motion !

Punch: Nature balances. Time speaks.

Advice: The Universe favors goodness & nothing can justify a wrong deed with negative intentions. It all comes back and this is the time for you to get results of your efforts.

Something Else: Analyze your deeds of the past. Tread with care, Karma is at its peak for you now.

JUSTICE

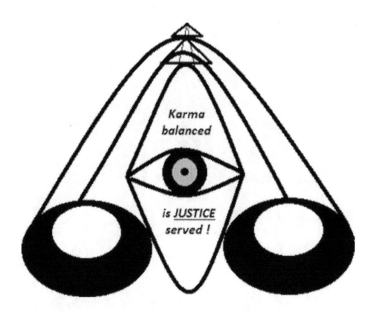

Punch: What's not working is not required.

Advice: Legal matters could be an issue for you. A break up, partition or divorce is indicated. Cut down on any habit which is harmful for you.

Something else: Dispose and do away with anything that is not in use. Clean, cleanse and simplify your life and surroundings.

HANGED MAN

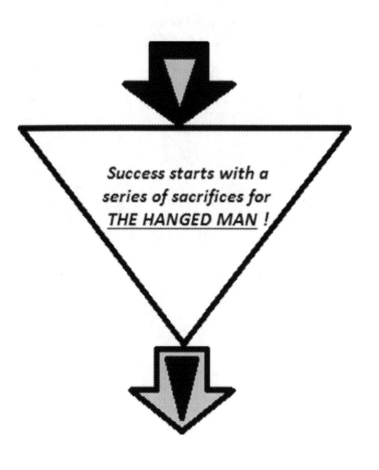

Success starts with a
series of sacrifices for
THE HANGED MAN !

Punch: You are a victim as long as you wish to be.

Advice: Adjust with situations, even if they are not pleasing at the moment. Nothing much can be done about them, except going with the flow. Look after your health and overall well being.

Something else: Take up creative activities like yoga, art classes, meditation, singing or aerobics.

DEATH

DEATH is not the
end, it is a new
beginning !

Punch: If your belief is outdated, let it die.

Advice: Renew, refresh, restart. Make changes before you are forced to change by circumstances beyond your power.

Something Else: A makeover is needed either physically, mentally, emotionally or spiritually. Do anything to change your attitude, your look, your image. It will bring a much required freshness to your existence.

Temperance

Allowing the process of growth to take it's natural course requires TEMPERANCE !

Punch: A heady mixture uses right proportions and ingredients.

Advice: This is not the time to cross boundaries. Staying within limits will yield great results.

Something else: Prepare salad with fruits or vegetables. Squeeze some fresh juice. Make yourself comfortable, have the salad and drink juice while thinking of the good things to come your way. A calm atmosphere with soothing light & incense is a bonus

DEVIL

Addictions and Cravings
empower *THE DEVIL*
to ensnare you !

Punch: A lesson is being taught, learn it.

Advice: All that is visible is not always the truth. There are unseen and unknown energies acting to divert your mind. There is a way out, it may not be so easy.

Something Else: Throw away anything that is not in use and is occupying your emotional and physical space. Letting go is the key word here.

TOWER

The strongest <u>TOWER</u> can break under immense pressure !

Punch: If ego is your power, then failure will be your teacher.

Advice: Avoid sudden actions or decisions. Being careful at every instance will be your savior. Tread carefully.

Something Else: Get a set of building blocks. Build and break it down again. Then rebuild again. Know that when life breaks you down, it will give you an opportunity to rebuild, just like the game.

STAR

Being <u>THE STAR</u> is not easy but it is not impossible either !

Punch: If you do not care, no one will.

Advice: Don't allow your goodness to diminish. Circumstances will be favorable after hard times are done with. Property matters will bring luck.

Something else: Water plants. Make a special place to keep water for animals and birds. Offer food and water to the needy.

Moon

THE MOON casts shadows that appear real !

Punch: The road exists, the path is lonely, the directions are many.

Advice: Not knowing what lies ahead and not being able to see the path clearly makes you insecure and uneasy. To clear this confusion, ask someone to help you.

Something Else: Take a break from your thoughts for 3 days. Stop yourself from planning, analyzing or thinking about the situation that is worrying you during this time. You will get clarity soon.

Sun

Everyone knows the power of

THE SUN !

Punch: Bliss is the goal. Harmony is the reward.

Advice: Family happiness is a gift, treasure it. Your children do well and prosper with your support and love.

Something Else: Plan a nice Sunday meal with your family and close relations in the afternoon. Happiness comes from being with loved ones.

JUDGMENT

_**JUDGMENT**
of Nature can never go
wrong !_

Punch: Rewards are not final, punishments are not fatal.

Advice: The past cannot change. The new karma you build should be a conscious effort to make a better future keeping the aspect of good deeds in mind.

Something Else: Don't judge, not yourself, not others. Concentrate on building a good future letting go of all that has gone wrong in the past.

WORLD

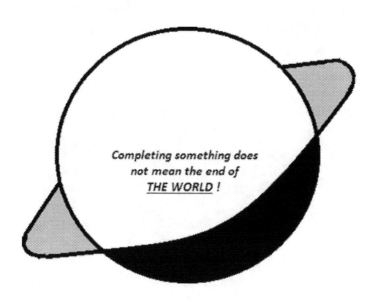

Completing something does not mean the end of <u>THE WORLD</u> !

Punch: Tasks culminated make space for new challenges.

Advice: A project is done and comes to completion. Travel to new places. A phase of life finishes, a fresh start is in the making.

Something Else: For 21 days, take time out and go for a walk or meditate or write the events of your days during this time. Know that a phase of life is going to alter.

THE MINOR ARCANA

Life is how we live it on a daily basis. Everyday makes a difference to our life as a whole. The importance and significance of this is represented by the Minor Arcana.

There are 4 Suits in the *Minor Arcana,* each having 10 pip(numbered cards) and 4 court cards making a total of 14 cards for each suit. The *Pip* cards relate to events and situations in a reading and advise us as to how to act or initiate a process.

The *Court* Cards that are pulled in your reading could either represent a character or a person of those qualities influencing your life, it could also denote yourself or an advice for you as to how you need to deal with the situation you are asking about.

I shall talk about each suit including all the cards that relate to it.

Wands

Wands represent the eternal flame of the Soul. The fire and the passion that burns within. On the negative side, too much fire can destroy any thing (animate or inanimate).

Positively wands in a reading influence your passion, energy, the intuitive side; making you active and energetic but you need to remember that too much fire can burn you out and make you lethargic and lazy.

Element: Fire

Time of the day: Afternoon

Health: Blood Pressure, Anger, Aggression

Ace Of Wands:

Advice: The feeling within is your guide, it is showing you a direction towards the right path. Do not ignore it. Your creativity is at it's peak, you are ready to work on your thoughts and ideas. Don't lose the moment.

2 Of Wands:

Advice: You have made up your mind, yet you are unsure as to whether it would be the right thing to do. Stall your plans till you are sure of yourself. Tough choices surround you, so waiting for clarity would be the right choice.

3 Of Wands:

Advice: Your wishes will be granted and you will take a step up in the ladder of success. Look for signs and opportunities that come your way. Be open to accepting challenges, they could be an opportunity in disguise that you have been waiting for.

4 Of Wands:

Advice: Focus on your family. Happy times are expected in your home. Give attention to detail, cleanliness and decorating your living space. Family functions and celebrations are around the corner.

5 Of Wands:

Advice: There are problems which could be created by you or by others around you. You will have to draw the line and understand how much you need to tolerate and when you need to fight back. The struggle is within you which is extending to the world outside(surrounding cards will clarify the meaning better).

6 Of Wands:

Advice: Your time will come even though the competition is tough. You have to see yourself as one of the tough competitors to achieve your goals. Success and victory after hard work is yours to enjoy.

7 Of Wands:

Advice: You cannot allow yourself to give up now even though things might not look easy from where you stand. This is not going to be your situation forever. Now is the time to stand strong on your beliefs.

8 Of Wands:

Advice: Seize this moment of movement, speed, communications and travel. You will say all the right things at the right time and impress the right people too. This won't last forever but the impact and impression you make on others at this time, definitely will.

9 Of Wands:

Advice: You need to stop your activities before you burn yourself out completely, maintain a routine and set a time table. There are obstacles to cross and you need to be sharp at this time. Conserve and reserve your energies till you are ready to start again.

10 Of Wands:

Advice: Drop everything that you are doing. Your efforts are being wasted so no point losing your energy on it. This time is not right for your ventures, working towards any of your goals will only tire and stress you out further. A feeling of lethargy might engulf you and make you feel powerless. Let this time pass and you will feel rejuvenated and renewed.

PRINCESS OF WANDS:

Character: A person who is easily angered and gets agitated with the smallest of issues, is quick to react and impatient in dealing with situations or people around, temperamental and career oriented.

Advice: Be impulsive when you have a great idea and put it into action before you lose interest in it. You can expect some news regarding your query. Avoid spicy food and drink water regularly.

PRINCE OF WANDS:

Character: A person who is determined to rise up in life and career and can take advantage of any situation given the opportunity. Can also use people as stepping stones for selfish motives.

Advice: A change with respect to job or career could be in the offing. Travel also proves beneficial. Expect news regarding promotion or a new job offer.

QUEEN Of WANDS:

Character: A person with great and immense authority who desires to be in power and wants to control any situation possible. This person could be a great director, advisor and leader. Taking charge of any and every event comes naturally to this personality.

Advice: It is time to execute your leadership qualities and use your ability to head your projects or life with complete dedication. Handling too many things at the same time might make you shun responsibility and leave things incomplete.

KING OF WANDS:

Character: The King of Wands exudes a persona of absolute brilliance and strength. Someone who is easily irritated at the slightest provocation. The king is aware of the effect his presence has around his surroundings. A person who has built his empire with his knowledge, will and ability, his experience makes him who and what he is.

Advice: Work with people, build relations, take charge of anything you see that could be slipping out of your hands. You know best how to make things work and bring them in your favor again.

Pentacles

Pentacles represent material possessions and valuables. They could also denote a position or designation that bring you material benefits and pleasures to keep up with your image in society.

Positively, pentacles will reflect career, status in society, financial status, possessions and property.

On a negative note, they denote greediness, attitude of hoarding and wanting material comforts in excess.

Element: Earth

Time Of Day: Night

Health: Bones, Teeth.

Ace Of Pentacles:

Advice: Act on your thought for the new business you want to start. You will reap the benefits of hard work and be suitably rewarded. This is a time of growth, initiating this process with the right attitude and willingness to work will bring rewards.

2 Of Pentacles:

Advice: Your situation might not look steady right now, this is not the time to squander money but wait. Weigh your options, changes are taking place behind the scenes that you might not be aware of. You need to take care of your health right now. A proposal for new business venture or career options will be made to you. Decide carefully.

3 Of Pentacles:

Advice: Co-operate with others and they will do so too. You will realize that you work better as a team now. There are people who appreciate you for your good work. Your name is on a list for promotion or for a new job offer.

4 Of Pentacles:

Advice: There will be increase in your status, personal and financial. Work related to property and building prove lucky. Concentrate on saving your income as of now. This is not the time to make any investments.

5 Of Pentacles:

Advice: There are differences in opinion that need to be sorted. Delay your decisions on financial matters. Your financial situation will improve, give it time. Do not get into unnecessary arguments with anyone.

6 Of Pentacles:

Advice: Recycle your good luck and it will bring you better luck. Giving will never reduce what you have, it will make space for you to get more. Donate to the right cause and help the needy, you will flourish and prosper with their blessings.

7 Of Pentacles:

Advice: The Universe works in a standard way of giving results after a time lapse. Be it a seed that is planted or a test that is given, there is always a wait-time to know how we fared. This wait period can be tiring and very frustrating, things are taking longer than usual to bear results, but that is how it is going to be for now.

8 Of Pentacles:

Advice: Apply your skills to your business, profession, career, home or anything you plan to undertake. You can look forward towards appreciation and great results for your hard work. Take up new skills, hobby classes, showcase your talent. Do things in a creative way.

9 Of Pentacles:

Advice: All that you have worked for is coming your way. Payments, property & matters that you have forgotten about or have let go of, that rightfully belong to you will be given to you in due time.

10 Of Pentacles:

Advice: Your family supports you financially and will come to your aid to fund your projects. Issues of inheritance & ancestral property need to be sorted. In times of difficulty, look for support and advice from your elders and trusted family members.

PRINCESS OF PENTACLES:

Character: A practical person who does not analyze or delve deeper into subjects. Someone who is not logical, is mathematical and materialistic. Outer appearances matter more than anything to this person who is attracted to places and products that enhance physical beauty.

Advice: Be patient, every situation needs time to build to bring results. You can expect some news regarding progress in work place or regarding career.

PRINCE OF PENTACLES:

Character: A person who believes in hard work and won't give up easily. This person has the ability to trust himself and his efforts and knows that he will reach his destination if he continues on his path. Sometimes this prince can become very rigid and stubborn that might create complications in relations.

Advice: Do things with complete faith and honesty and believe that you will get positive results. Not deviating from your path and not listening to the doubts created in your mind or by others will work in your favor.

QUEEN OF PENTACLES:

Character: This person loves being visible in social circles and gatherings. Someone who appreciates beauty and art in all forms and will go out of their way to promote talent keeping their own monetary interest in mind.

Advice: You will be successful in any business venture you undertake. Take up creative activities and learn new forms of art or talent, anything that interests you. Your knowledge will help you in the future. Stay grounded while you are being appreciated for your hard work and efforts. Do not allow yourself to be fooled by false praise.

KING OF PENTACLES:

Character: This king is very good with monetary matters and handles finances really well. A person who has a keen sense of business and has the ability to build an empire from scratch. Someone who feels responsible as a provider for their family and workers alike.

Advice: You are moving in the right direction with your decisions and have the ability to deal with any crisis that comes along the way. Finances need to be handled with care. Save your income and invest wisely, it will bring profits.

CUPS

Cups as the name suggests is a vessel that carries the weight of our emotional and spiritual feelings.

On a positive level, being emotional and attuned to others' feeling will give us an upper hand in understanding ourselves and others, always doing the right thing on a karmic level.

Negatively, being too caring and giving can overwhelm us and leave us with very little time for ourselves.

Element: Water

Time Of The Day: Dawn

Health: Emotional Issues, Love, Spiritual, Water borne diseases

Ace Of Cups:

Advice: The soul seeks a spiritual bond and connection to make you feel desired and cared for. You need to focus on what you are and not what you have become over a period of time with experience. Recognise and appreciate yourself for the loving being you are.

2 Of Cups:

Advice: Merging of different beings, organisations or companies strengthen the partnership. Co-operation and communication bring togetherness. Romance and love is highlighted for you.

3 Of Cups:

Advice: Love what you do and do what you love. Nothing brings greater joy when you have immense faith in yourself and everyone who supports you. Hope for the best but stay grounded at the same time. Don't overspend in a rush of emotions.

4 Of Cups:

Advice: Think and analyse. Your emotional well being depends on your soul's ability to be happy. It is not always about owning material goods but being content about what you have. Relationships prove stressful.

5 Of Cups:

Advice: Looking back will weaken your next step as your focus is not on what lies ahead but on what you left behind. Don't make it difficult for yourself to move on, it has to be done for your own sanity. Blaming yourself or others will only make you sad and unhappy.

6 Of Cups:

Advice: The best days in life are those spent in innocence, knowing that there is nothing you need to worry about. Remember the happy days of your childhood, with your family and friends and recreate the magic of those days by meeting them, talking on the phone and having a good time.

7 Of Cups:

Advice: Prioritize your life. Simply thinking about all the things you need to do will not help. It will stress you out further. Set out to complete one thing at a time and you will feel relaxed which will enable you to accomplish other goals that you have set for yourself.

8 Of Cups:

Advice: Leave everything you are doing and leave it now. Crying or being depressed about how you have been treated by your loved ones will not solve anything. Get up and change your image, go to the parlor, get a makeover. Bring fresh energy for yourself. Value yourself and you will be valued by all.

9 Of Cups:

Advice: What you want will be given to you. Wishes will be granted, prayers will be fulfilled. Blessings coming your way are unlimited. There is goodwill about you and it will manifest into positive results.

10 Of Cups:

Advice: A beautiful home, a happy family and a prosperous life look possible; your spirituality, karma and good deeds have brought you closer to emotional well being and happiness where you meet everyone with love and joy.

PRINCESS OF CUPS:

Character: This is a person with a poetic bend, very sensitive and vulnerable who loves to be around people and makes friends with ease. The need to be appreciated by everyone is strong in them. They have a great sense of music and acting abilities.

Advice: Be aware of how much you need to sacrifice for others and not overdo anything to get praise and appreciation. Write your thoughts and emotions on paper. Taking up creative activities will be a good channel to let out your emotional frustrations.

PRINCE OF CUPS:

Character: A charmer who has the ability to attract everyone and is very dexterous with words. They know what makes others tick and can mould themselves with everyone and fit with the crowd. This person knows how to get their way with people and anyone can be easily fooled with their flamboyant personality.

Advice: A proposal is on it's way. Don't rush into a relationship, it could just be a passing phase or maybe someone has taken your fancy and it is momentary. Do not trust anyone on the basis of their spoken word, let actions be proof to their loyalty and commitment.

QUEEN OF CUPS:

Character: A mature, well spoken, sensitive and sensible person who knows what to say and when. This person understands others too well and knows how to turn anything in their own favor when the time is right. They can make good advisors and have a natural ability to help people.

Advice: Don't get too involved in others' problems that you start to neglect yourself and your family. Know who is your well wisher and do not get influenced by those who show their blind support to you, they might have ulterior, long term motives that might not be favorable to you.

KING OF CUPS:.

Character: A person with a sense of pride that can falter if not checked. Someone who has authority and control over their emotions and are prone to keeping their hurt and anger buried within themselves for years altogether. They can be very unforgiving and carry grudges for a long time.

Advice: Speak and communicate with your family and loved ones. Share problems and doubts instead of constantly thinking about them and adding to your stress. Stop cursing others for your own vulnerability and for not being able to see their reality sooner.

SWORDS

Swords are suits that operate on a mental level, deal with thoughts and our mind. To change any situation, we need to change the way we perceive it; once that is done, we can look for different ways to approach anything that we aim to achieve.

Ace Of Swords:

Advice: Speak your mind, ask questions and get rid of those doubts that are hounding you. Your ability to talk and confront a situation that is bothering you will act as your defense system this time.

2 Of Swords:

Advice: Just because you cannot see something does not mean it does not exist, you maybe subconsciously trying to avoid looking at a situation because you want to believe the best. But you will need to face the truth, sooner or later.

3 Of Swords:

Advice: A feeling of unhappiness engulfs you and it is so strong that you are not able to think or work straight. Things have gone awry and haywire and your sorrow is a result of heart break and interference of others in your life. It will be a long time before you overcome this phase if you do not consciously make an effort to stay happy.

4 Of Swords:

Advice: You are tired and need to withdraw from anything or anyone that is making you sick or draining your energy. Take a break or go on a vacation. Your main concern right now is to heal and regain your positive thoughts to be able to get back into action.

5 Of Swords:

Advice: Thinking will not change anything and over-thinking will distress you even further. This is not the time to take any action or retaliate, you will not get results and it will be a wasted effort. Seeking help and solace in spirituality and prayers is a good thing to do.

6 Of Swords:

Advice: Everyone faces hardships, you are going through one of your own storms. This phase in your life requires you to remain positive, no matter how difficult it is, the good phase will be restored and you will see progress in matters, give it time.

7 Of Swords:

Advice: Planning and plotting against others has led to your downfall. Keeping people by your side only because you have an agenda to fulfill will knock you off your feet. If your intentions are not right, your plans will backfire.

8 Of Swords:

Advice: If you are doubtful about a situation, you are probably right in your thinking. The only way out is to be curious and find out more about what you are getting into before committing yourself to a project or person.

9 Of Swords:

Advice: The tough and the bad phase of your life are coming to end but not before you have faced them and dealt with them. This will be time consuming and traumatic. There will be undue pressure on your mind and an uneasiness that you need to deal with to clear your path for further progress.

10 Of Swords:

Advice: You feel as if everyone is out to get you, your sensitivity is at it's peak and somehow you are absorbing negative vibes from anything and anyone who you come in contact with. Distance yourself from the outside world. The best way out of this phase is to focus on yourself, your health and your over all well being. Seek help if the situation gets unbearable.

PRINCESS OF SWORDS:

Character: A talkative person who has the ability to give you a lot of information but nothing of value. Someone who loves to gossip and play mind games, is tech savvy and uses electronics with ease.

Advice: You would do well in a career that requires quick thinking, talking and conversing. You have the gift of the gab as they call it. Working in fields that require dealing with people and places from other countries will be in your favor.

PRINCE OF SWORDS:

Character: This is a person who does not like to waste time and is quick to take action on every thought and idea to make it work for them. These people fight for a just cause, be it for themselves or others.

Advice: This is the moment to take charge of your situation, your goals are within reach. You have the ability, knowledge and tact to fight for a social and just cause to help the distressed.

QUEEN OF SWORDS:

Character: A single person with a high level of intelligence. This card represents a person who expects perfection in everything and does not believe in spoon feeding. A self-made person with great dignity and finesse, this person does not believe in talking but working hard to prove their worth. Being able to catch on to any nuance behind spoken words and being direct in speech is a special quality this queen exhibits.

Advice: Make sure you are not getting caught up by outer appearances since they can be deceptive. Be direct in your conversations to make a point and your approach will be appreciated. Before starting a project, look into details and eliminate excess, unnecessary procedures.

KING OF SWORDS:

Character: A level headed personality with authority and control, someone with a balanced mind holding strong opinions. People look up to this king for advice. This person might come across as detached and unapproachable.

Advice: You will make a good lawyer, advisor and mediator. Do not alienate yourself and try to associate with others instead of living on a mental plane. Your ideas are appreciated, put them into action and work on them.

How a beginner should approach the Tarot Cards.

- Start by doing one card readings. Each card has a specific meaning and they change depending on other cards pulled out with them. Hence, start on a small scale and work on one card at a time for better understanding and connection with tarot.

- Before reading for others, practice a lot. Remember that counseling and guiding is a job of great responsibility. People will look up to you for directing them to the right path and making decisions. For that, you need to be good at your work and start with daily readings for yourself.

- Pick a card at the beginning of your day and set it aside (either mentally or physically) and get along with your routine. At the end of the day, review the events of your day, then relate it to the card you had picked up, this will help you to relate with the cards.

- Never repeatedly ask the same question to your cards. It is human nature to doubt the answers we receive. You want to hear or read what you think will work for you. Keep in mind that cards have an energy of their own, they will guide you with respect to the most important aspect of your life, about the things you need to know, to become aware of your situation or anything you have been neglecting and avoiding.

- Some times, you might pick cards that seem totally irrelevant to your question. These cards are telling you a step-by-step procedure of how to reach your goals. It just means you have to follow a particular path and go through a series of events to attain what you are asking for.

- Tarot Cards have an energy of their own, they are sacred and should be treated and consulted with utmost care. Keeping your cards in special cases or wrapped in special cloth will enhance the energy of your cards and help in better readings.

- Give your cards a break-time. When you are constantly pulling the same card over and over again, keep your cards aside and focus on other things or some other deck. Your cards are not ready to reply to your query specially if the other deck you use also gives you similar cards. Do not consult your cards for a week to 10 days or seek help from a professional, if your situation demands it.

THE KEY TO READING CARDS

1. The first thing any reader should notice is the suits that appear in any spread or reading. That suit will overpower and change the meaning of the reading.

2. Reading single cards is advisable for beginners but we cannot completely depend on them for detailed readings. As and when the reader becomes experienced, it will be important to combine cards and their meanings.

3. Avoid **YES** and **NO** spreads. Those are childish games. This is not a flower you can pick up and ask questions like *s/he loves me*, *s/he loves me not* and then you get your answer depending on the final petal of the flower. There are a lot of other factors that play a role in determining the happening of an event. Using spreads with multiple cards help to get a clearer picture.

4. Book meanings are a guide with traditional value attached to each card. However, nothing can replace pure intuition when you see the cards. The first impression and thought when seeing a card is of great importance. Combining your knowledge with your intuition while reading a card is a good way to start predicting.

MAY BE SPREAD

Expecting an answer in black and white while consulting The Tarot is natural. However, you will not get such clarity *always* as there are many factors that need to be considered for the future you are asking about.

Tarot is not the final answer as many would like to believe, it shows us a way ahead for the nearest possibility of the occurrence of an event. Your inputs and your efforts also determine how you can change a situation to your liking or alter the result depending on your approach.

For this reason, a YES/NO spread should always be accompanied by a MAYBE card which tells you if you need to apply your own energy and effort for better results.

While picking cards, place them face down in their respective position on the spread. Open each card and place it face up one at a time. Look for strong cards and see which position they occupy. This will answer your query as to where you are heading on your path and how close you are to attaining your goal.

Example of a MAYBE Spread

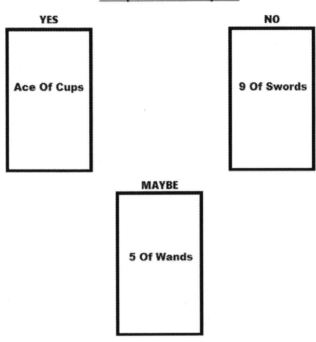

YES

Ace Of Cups

NO

9 Of Swords

MAYBE

5 Of Wands

Interpretation of the Maybe Spread:

In the spread, the inquirer has drawn 3 cards for each position.
Yes is occupied by Ace Of Cups.
No is occupied by 9 Of Swords.
Maybe is occupied by 5 Of Wands.

This spread is a clear indication that whatever the inquirer is asking for will come about and there will be success. However, if we take the same cards and change their places, the answer will also change.

Variations:

If the card, 9 Of Swords would occupy the **YES** position on the spread, then the inquirer's answer would be No !
If the card, Ace Of Cups would occupy the **MAYBE** position, then the inquirer should know that there are many other factors that are involved in the situation being asked about and that there is a possibility of it happening, if everything else is taken into consideration.

Preparing for a reading:

1. Create a special space where you read your cards.
2. Light a candle, incense sticks or use a special ritual like meditation/breathing exercises before a reading.
3. Keep a special cloth that you use only to keep or spread your cards on. Do not mix other clothes with your reading cloth.
4. Energize and attune your cards by holding them in your hands and mentally asking them to help you with your reading.
5. Ring a bell on the cards thrice to clear any previous energies the cards have collected.
6. You can keep lucky charms or pictures and statues of your deity in your reading space.
7. Keep your mind free from any other thought while reading cards so you do not mix your personal feelings with the card meanings.

Points to be noted:

- Your cards are your best friend, they will not tell you things to please you but will disclose information that will help you. Treat them with care.

- You can always carry your cards along with you, however, it is always good to keep them in a special pouch.

- Cards have a powerful energy of their own, they might create disturbance in your sleep patterns if they are kept around you at night.

- Speak with your cards as you would speak to your friend and they will respond and communicate with you in their own way.

- Love your cards, you will feel their magic around you.

- Always give yourself a break between readings, this will help you clear energies that you pick up from others or from your space.

- Reading Tarot should not be restricted to interpreting images on cards but also relate to numerology, planets, astrology, occult and science.

SPELL CASTING

A lot of my clients and others have asked me if they should cast spells to achieve their desires, this is a good platform to address issues regarding the subject.

Spell casting is serious business and is not a child's play. Before casting a spell, you need to understand that a spell has the ability to back fire and go wrong if you are not careful.

A few things need to be considered before you work with spells:

1. Phase of the Moon
2. Time of the Day
3. Day of the Week
4. What you are asking for
5. How you have worded the spell
6. The intensity with which you cast the spell

JUSTICE SPELL

Before doing this, you must remember that such a spell will not only bring justice to you but will also look at your actions and karma that make you accountable for any wrong that you have done, intentionally or unintentionally. Think carefully before planning to cast any spell.

This is a very good spell for those who are made to feel hopeless and are on the verge of giving up on everything. It will revive their strength and heal them from any negative situation being created in their lives.

Ingredients:

1) Sea Salt, about 2 hand full
2) 4 Purple Candles

Method:

This spell is to be done for 4 consecutive Wednesdays preferably during the evening or night time. Or select a time that is comfortable for you and stick to it.

Method:

Cleanse and sweep a part of the North-West of your space, room, home or office; place a metal dish there, taking care of safety. Put some sea salt in the metal dish in a circular form. Place a purple candle in the centre and focus on the situation where injustice is being done to you. Light this candle and let it burn out knowing that your issue is being taken care of by the Universe while the candle melts. Let Go.

The next day, take the sea salt and pour it in some water body, imagining the stress leaving you.

Repeat this for 3 more Wednesdays. You will gradually start to feel positive and be at peace regarding the situation that is bothering you.

CLARITY SPELL

The mind is always clouded with constant analyzing and thinking. This makes your situation even more blurry and creates confusion which will in turn impair the decision you take or not allow you to make a decision at all.

At such times, casting a spell for gaining clarity can be helpful.

Ingredients:

1) 1 piece of white sheet
2) 1 piece of black sheet
3) 1 black marker
4) 1 white marker
5) A bottle of water
6) Glass to pour water

Method:

Collect all these items and go to a quiet place either in your home or outdoors. Calm yourself. Then pour water in a glass and drink it, gathering your thoughts. On the black sheet of paper, with a white marker, write all the negative thoughts about the situation that is creating a confusion for you. Read this paper and fold it. Keep it aside.

Then, on the white sheet of paper with black marker, write down all the positive feelings you have about the situation. Read it and fold it.

Hold both these sheets in the palms of your hands. Close your eyes and allow your thoughts to flow. Imagine that your thoughts are flowing out of you and into the white and black sheet of papers. After you feel comfortable, open your eyes, drink water if you feel the need. Tear the sheets imagining yourself doing away with the confusion. Do not think about the situation for a few days. You will gain clarity or help with it in someway.

YOUR SIGNATURE

The way you sign has a great impact on your life and you as a whole. Your signature not only defines you as a person but also the life events and planetary influences acting upon you.

You can follow some simple methods to enhance your persona through the way you sign:

- Your signature should always have an upward flow, this denotes success and positive movement towards progress.

- Avoid having a signature that breaks in the middle, it signifies stagnation or a sudden stall in events in the projects you undertake.

- Your signature should be clear and well defined.

- Avoid having negative signs in your signature such as a minus sign(-) or a downward arrow, it denotes downfall.

SIGNATURE POWER SPELL

Many times, you might feel like you have lost control of your life, try this simple method to get your thoughts together and take charge of your life again.

Items required:

1) 10 sheets of paper or a book.
2) A pen with red ink

Method:

For 10 days, practice your signature on paper. Do this till you fill the paper up. After that is done, look at this paper for a few minutes and breathe in, feeling the positive vibes.

You will feel energized and in a better frame of mind once you complete this exercise.

MEDITATION

Meditation is the purest form of healing and bringing joy and peace in our lives. However, it gets boring for a lot of people who do not understand how to concentrate or follow breathing exercises without their mind being diverted by different thoughts.

That is the reason, Rainbow meditation is simple to follow while it brings healing and peace to the person.

RAINBOW MEDITATION AND AURA CLEANSING SPELL

Rainbow meditation is a special type of meditation which focuses on the colors of the rainbow, VIBGYOR -> Violet, Indigo, Blue, Green, Yellow, Orange and Red.

The 7 main chakras of the physical body are also aligned with these colors. Rainbow meditation is a way to energize these chakras to allow them to function well which in turn will help the body to stay healthy.

Method:

Choose a time of the day when you will not be disturbed. Switch off your phones. Sit or lie down in a place you feel comfortable.

Once you feel at ease. Close your eyes and imagine yourself surrounded by a ball of white light. Keep breathing in and out during this whole process.

After a few minutes, imagine the while light turn into Violet, keep breathing, inhale and exhale.

Repeat this process imagining the colors change, from Violet to Indigo to Blue to Green to Yellow to Orange and then Red.

Once you have completed the process of imagining all the colors, it is time for closure. Imagine the color Red finally turn to a White ball of light. Stay with this for a few minutes and open your eyes slowly.

You will feel refreshed and positive. Do this meditation once or twice a week and you will regain good health and be able to stay positive. This will also helps in cleansing your aura from negativities that you pick from interaction with others.

ADVANCED UNDERSTANDING OF TAROT

Many believe and have a preconceived notion that reading Tarot requires interpretation of cards by learning their meaning and looking at images. It is just a small part of Tarot.

Tarot is much more than that. My study of Tarot has revealed to me that you can relate it with anything scientific, occult or spiritual.

Tarot and Numerology

The numbered cards of Tarot reveal a greater significance on how they have been associated with the cards.

Having more knowledge about numbers and their behavior will strengthen the readings. Your date of birth also reveals your personal card which will help you to understand your future and your own being.

Something to be noted:

- All the pip cards with the number 5 do not have pleasant attributes attached with them.

- All cards with the number 6 are positive.

Tarot and Astrology

Every card is influenced by certain qualities of planets. This helps you in understanding your planetary situation accurately. Even if you do not have your own birth chart which also requires your date of birth and place of birth, a tarot reading will guide you in the best possible manner.

Tarot and Spirituality

The cards have a great spiritual significance and denote a journey. In this case, it is that of an innocent who learns and understands material and spiritual values, overcomes obstacles and finally reaches the destination.

A complete path is outlined by the cards of the Major Arcana where The Fool starts off on his quest with belief and hope, learns the tricks and trade, understands about mystical forces and other worldly affairs to become an individual while making choices to reach where he wants to go.

Every card has spiritual significance and also deals with the soul and it's journey. These cards also help to understand that even if the situation does not look smooth on a physical level, there could be an underlying spiritual growth and progress taking place, which is important for our soul and life path.

Tarot and Nature

Nature is complete with the 5 elements - Earth, Fire, Water, Air and Ether. These are denoted by the elements which represent the Minor Arcana and Ether(the essence) by the Major Arcana.

Tarot is a natural tool that addresses our concerns of life, be it a daily issue or something that needs to be dealt with on a larger level.

The most natural human quality is to question and be curious as to why things happen. Tarot cards have a natural ability to answer these queries. They are the best guides that can direct you with complete honesty through your own ability or that of a reader.

Interpreting Tarot

Cards don't lie. It totally depends on the reader who interprets them on how accurate a reading will be.

To be a good reader, you have to work on yourself without giving up.

This requires:

- A daily schedule of working with cards

- Regular meditation

- Nature walks and cleansing the chakras of your body (refer Rainbow Meditation)

- Cleansing your aura (refer Rainbow Meditation)

- Cleansing your cards after every reading

- Cleansing your reading space

- Having an intention to help and do good for those who seek guidance

How to deal with clients

While reading for others, keep in mind the following:

1. You are resolving issues for others, take something in exchange. If you do not feel comfortable keeping

money given to you, donate it to charity or use it for a good cause.

2. People can take advantage of the fact that you can help them. They will move on with their lives once they get their answers. Be detached and do not expect to make contacts because of your ability to read cards.

3. Do not read for clients without their permission. Being nosy and curious about anyone's life is not a good thing and it implies using your ability for your own intentions.

4. Ask your clients to follow up and give their feed back so you know about your reading and this will also help you to deal with the situation further, if need be.

5. Do not waste your spirituality and power on people who do not respect you, your ability and the Tarot, in general.

6. Be fair while reading cards for others. Keep your own thoughts and advice aside while answering queries.

THE LAST PAGE

Someone once signed on the last page of my scrap book. It said *Never neglect the last page* and that has been embedded in my mind since then.

So last but not the least, I wish to thank God, The Highest Power, my spiritual angels and guides for the protection they provided to me, the intuitive powers that came from them which I have ignored at many times, the courage I got from them to keep moving on my path towards success even though I wanted to give in and break down on many occasions.

My close knit family for giving me a life of comfort and freedom to go after my dreams.

My mother, Gurjinder Mehta- I cannot describe her inputs in my life, no words can match her tolerance and patience with me!

My father, Jitendra Nath Mehta for having faith in my cards and readings and blessing me at all times to be a successful human!

My sister, Shuchi, whose presence, prayers and support have taken off a lot of burdens off my shoulder!

Thank you, Mandeep Kwatra, for helping me with the book cover, you are truly a blessing for us all!

I love you all even though I might not say it often!

My pets, the ones who are with me and the ones who have moved to another plane, they have brought joy, laughter and happiness in my life! My late pet mouse would actually pick cards and hand them to me, I cannot forget the lessons taught to me during her time with me!

I love my clients and specially those who gradually turned into my friends! Thank you for standing by me. It is amazing how well you have managed to deal with me and adjust with my personalities - Treating me as a guide and counselor when you seek help and as a friend at other casual moments! You are the ones who I first shared about my new venture, your offer to help me with my book means a lot to me!

I am grateful to be guided by the Universal energies towards fulfillment of my goals and thank the stars and heavens for directing me to my publishers!!!

Yours truly,

Nisha Mehta